MW00748874

These pages may be copied.

Permission is granted to the buyer of this book to reproduce, duplicate or photocopy these materials for use with students in Sunday school or Bible teaching classes.

Rainbow Books

Rainbow Publishers • P.O. Box 261129 • San Diego, CA 92196

Jennifer Nystrom

For my three children, Matthew, Erik and Amy, who prove to me day after day that God can use even the youngest of us for His glory.

FAVORITE BIBLE CHILDREN FOR AGES 4&5
©2000 by Rainbow Publishers, second printing
ISBN 1-885358-76-8
Rainbow reorder# RB36912

Rainbow Publishers
P.O. Box 261129
San Diego, CA 92196

Illustrator: Chuck Galey
Cover Illustrator: Helen Lannis
Editor: Christy Allen

Scriptures are from the *Holy Bible: New International Version* (North American Edition), ©1973, 1978, 1984 by the International Bible Society. Used by permission of Zondervan Bible Publishers.

Printed in the United States of America

Table of Contents

Memory Verse Index 7

Introduction 9

Note to Parents 11

Isaac (Genesis 22:1-8)

I...I...Isaac 13

Blessing Door Knob Hanger 14

Isaac Puppet 16

God Provides a Ram 18

My Favorite Things..19

Where Is It? 20

Miriam (Exodus 1:22-2:10)

M...M...Miriam 21

Baby Watching Binoculars 22

Berry Basket Baby 23

See the Little Baby? 25

Love Never Fails 27

Find the Baby 29

Samuel (1 Samuel 2:18-19; 3:1-21)

S...S...Samuel 31

A Robe for Samuel 32

I Listen with My Ears 33

Make a Promise Keeper 35

What's That Sound? 37

Your Servant Is Listening 38

The Widow's Sons (2 Kings 4:1-7)

Mystery of the Missing Jar 39

Jars of Hope 40

Find the Twin Jars..42

Jar Full of Miracles..43

Puppet Sons...44

Naaman's Servant Girl (2 Kings 5:1-16)

Walk in the Way of the Lord 45

Little Servant Girl 46

Naaman's Obedience Walk 47

Obey the Lord 48

David the Shepherd Boy (1 Samuel 17:34-37)

D...D...David 49

David Protects His Sheep 50

Chain of Protection 51

Veggie Creatures 53

We Are God's Sheep 54

David and Goliath (1 Samuel 17:4-51)

The Lord's Battle 55

Count to Five 57

Five Stones of Faith 58

Collage of Trust 60

Trust and Obey 62

Jesus (Luke 2:41-52)

J...J...Jesus 63

Blow Painting Maze 64

Is That You, Jesus? 65

Jesus Is Here; Can You Find Him? 66

Jairus' Daughter (Mark 5:21-24; 35-43)

A Little Girl Is Healed 67

Circle the Differences 69

Don't Be Afraid 70

Search for the Words 71

Rag Doll and Bed 72

Jesus Loves, Jesus Heals 74

Boy and His Lunch (John 6:5-14; 25-40)

To Share Is to Love..76

Count How Many 78

Fishy Concentration Game 79

Loaf and Fish Mobile 81

Bread of Life..83

Share-a-Snack 84

What's for Lunch? 86

Timothy (1 Timothy 4:12; 2 Timothy 1:5-7; 3:14-15)

T...T...Timothy 88

"Love"ly Flowers 89

Grow as You Learn 90

Listen to Your Mother! 92

Memory Verse Choir..93

Thank You Letter 95

Memory Verse Index

Old Testament

Genesis 22:14 Isaac Puppet 16
God Provides a Ram 18
My Favorite Things................19
Where Is It?.........................20

Genesis 22:17 I…I…Isaac 13
Blessing Door Knob Hanger..14

1 Samuel 2:19 A Robe For Samuel................32

1 Samuel 3:10 I Listen with My Ears 33
Make a Promise Keeper 35
Your Servant Is Listening 38

1 Samuel 16:7 S…S…Samuel 31
What's That Sound? 37

1 Samuel 17:47 The Lord's Battle 55
Count to Five........................57

Psalm 27:1 M…M…Miriam 21
Baby Watching Binoculars 22
See the Little Baby? 25

Psalm 37:3 David Protects His Sheep 50
We Are God's Sheep 54
Five Stones of Faith 58
Collage of Trust 60
Trust and Obey 62

Psalm 37:5 Little Servant Girl 46

Psalm 128:1 Walk in the Way of the Lord..45
Naaman's Obedience Walk 47
Obey the Lord 48

Proverbs 3:5 Count How Many 78
Share-a-Snack 84

New Testament

Mark 5:36 Search for the Words 71
Don't Be Afraid 70
Rag Doll and Bed 72

Mark 5:41 A Little Girl is Healed 67
Circle the Differences.............69
Jesus Loves, Jesus Heals 74

Luke 2:44 Blow Painting Maze 64
Jesus is Here; Can You Find Him? ..66
Searching For Jesus 69

Luke 2:52 J…J…Jesus............................63
Is That You, Jesus? 65

John 6:35 To Share Is to Love.................76
Fishy Concentration Game 79
Loaf and Fish Mobile 81
Bread of Life..........................83
What's for Lunch? 86

Romans 15:13 Mystery of the Missing Jar......39
Jars of Hope 40
Find the Twin Jars..................42
Jar Full of Miracles.................43
Puppet Sons 44

1 Cor. 13:8 Berry Basket Baby 23
Love Never Fails.....................27
Find the Baby 29

1 Cor. 16:13 D…D…David............................49
Chain of Protection.................51
Veggie Creatures.....................53

2 Timothy 3:15 Grow as You Learn 90
Thank You Letter 95

1 Timothy 4:12 T…T…Timothy 88
"Love"ly Flowers 89
What Will I Be When I Grow Up? ..96

2 Timothy 1:7 Memory Verse Choir...............93

2 Timothy 3:14 Listen to Your Mother.............92

Introduction

No one is too young to begin learning about God and His great power and love. Not only can young children learn, they can be an example for other believers. Paul says in 1 Timothy 4:12: "Don't let anyone look down on you because you are young, but set an example for the believers in speech, in life, in love, in faith and in purity." God sees our hearts, not our ages.

Throughout the Bible there are numerous examples of children and young people making a difference. The Lord Himself chose to come to earth as a baby. What better way to teach young children about God than to use other children as examples! The crafts, games, puzzles and activities in *Favorite Bible Children* are designed to let children know that they can be instruments of God.

Each activity includes:

√ **Bible child's name or identifier**

√ **lesson title:** highlighting a Bible story

√ **Scripture reference:** for Bible story

√ **memory verse:** to reinforce the story, lesson or activity

√ **What You Need:** a materials list for the lesson

√ **What to Do:** how to conduct the activity

√ **What to Say:** a short lesson

The memory verse index on page 7 will help you match lessons to other Bible-teaching tools or curriculum you are using. To help keep activity costs to a minimum, send home the reproducible Note to Parents on page 11 to request help in gathering supplies. And remember: all patterns may be duplicated. You only need to buy one book for your entire class!

These crafts and activities focus on just a few of the children whose stories are recorded in the Bible. It was because these children were willing to be used by God and were obedient to Him that God was able to do great things through them. Whether their actions facilitated a miracle such as the little boy sharing his lunch with Jesus or the encouragement of others as with Timothy, God was able to use them because they loved and honored Him. Your young children are just starting to learn about God. Use *Favorite Bible Children* to teach them that no matter how young they are, God can use them.

To Families of 4 and 5 Year Olds,
We have some exciting activities planned for use in teaching Bible lessons this year. Some of these crafts and projects utilize ordinary household items. We'd like to ask your help in saving these items for our activities:

❏ cotton swabs
❏ adhesive bandages
❏ bags, paper grocery
❏ construction paper
❏ cornmeal
❏ cotton balls
❏ craft sticks
❏ curling ribbon, yellow and orange
❏ fabric scraps
❏ fish crackers
❏ gift wrap
❏ glitter
❏ jars, empty pickle

❏ lace, ribbon and yarn scraps
❏ old magazines
❏ old newspapers
❏ paper clips
❏ paper plates, dinner and dessert size
❏ paper sacks, lunch size
❏ peanuts, unshelled and unsalted
❏ plastic berry baskets
❏ plastic drinking straws
❏ rubber bands
❏ star stickers
❏ toilet paper tubes
❏ toothpicks

Please bring the items on _____
Thank you for your help!

To Families of 4 and 5 Year Olds,
We have some exciting activities planned for use in teaching Bible lessons this year. Some of these crafts and projects utilize ordinary household items. We'd like to ask your help in saving these items for our activities:

❏ cotton swabs
❏ adhesive bandages
❏ bags, paper grocery
❏ construction paper
❏ cornmeal
❏ cotton balls
❏ craft sticks
❏ curling ribbon, yellow and orange
❏ fabric scraps
❏ fish crackers
❏ gift wrap
❏ glitter
❏ jars, empty pickle

❏ lace, ribbon and yarn scraps
❏ old magazines
❏ old newspapers
❏ paper clips
❏ paper plates, dinner and dessert size
❏ paper sacks, lunch size
❏ peanuts, unshelled and unsalted
❏ plastic berry baskets
❏ plastic drinking straws
❏ rubber bands
❏ star stickers
❏ toilet paper tubes
❏ toothpicks

Please bring the items on _____
Thank you for your help!

Isaac

Memory Verse

I will surely bless you.
~Genesis 22:17

What You Need

- duplicated page
- crayons

What to Do

After reviewing the story, give each child a duplicate of this page. Tell them that Isaac's name begins with the letter I. Repeat the I sound together. Have the children circle the items on the page that begin with the letter I.

What to Say

Isaac loved God and he knew that his father loved God. They both wanted to do whatever it was that He asked of them. When God asked Abraham to sacrifice Isaac, they didn't question God. They were willing to obey no matter what. God saw how much they honored and loved Him and provided a way for them to worship Him without sacrificing Isaac. When we obey God and do what He wants us to do, even if we might not like it, we are showing Him that we love Him. Have you ever been asked to do something you really didn't want to do? Did you do it?

13

Isaac

Blessing Door Knob Hanger
৩ Genesis 22:1-18 ৩

Memory Verse

I will surely bless you.
~Genesis 22:17

What You Need

- page 15, duplicated
- card stock
- crayons or markers
- safety scissors

What to Do

Duplicate the pattern for the doorknob hanger from page 15 onto card stock. Have the children decorate them with crayons or markers and cut them out. Show how to cut out the hole for hanging.

What to Say

When Abraham and Isaac went up on the mountain, God saw that Abraham was willing to sacrifice his only son. He knew that Abraham must love Him more than his son. Both Abraham and Isaac showed their love for God through their obedience to Him, no matter what it was that God asked of them. They may not have even understood why God asked them to do this. Because they were obedient, God promised to bless them and all their descendants. Use your doorknob hanger at home to remind you of God's promise to us.

I will surely bless you.

Genesis 22:17

Isaac

Isaac Puppet
ᔓ Genesis 22:1-18 ᔓ

Memory Verse

The Lord will provide.
~Genesis 22:14

What You Need

- page 17, duplicated
- lunch-size paper bags
- glue sticks
- safety scissors
- crayons

What to Do

Have the children color and cut out both puppet pieces. With the lunch bag laying flat, show how to glue piece 1 to the bottom of the bag. Then the students should lift the bottom and glue piece 2 under the flap to make the mouth. When the children have finished their puppets, allow them to act out the Bible story.

What to Say

Isaac loved God and his father very much. Even though he must have wondered why God would want his father to sacrifice him, he was willing to obey. He knew that God must have a plan. Both Abraham and Isaac showed their faith and love for God in their obedience. Because of this, God provided a ram for them to sacrifice instead.

Piece #1

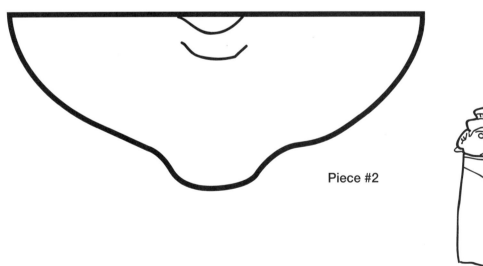

Piece #2

finished puppet

Isaac

God Provides a Ram
♪ Genesis 22:1-18 ♪

Memory Verse

The Lord will provide.
~Genesis 22:14

What You Need

- duplicated page
- crayons
- safety scissors
- paper fasteners

What to Do

Have the children color the bush and the ram and cut them out on the dotted lines. Show how to place the bush on top of the ram and fasten the two together with a paper fastener. The ram should peek out from behind the bush.

What to Say

God's provision of the ram in the thicket is just one example of how much God loves and provides for us. Abraham and Isaac probably found many things that they could use while they were on the mountain. But God knew they needed a sacrifice. Abraham was willing to make the ultimate sacrifice for God. God saw his love and faith and provided a ram for them.

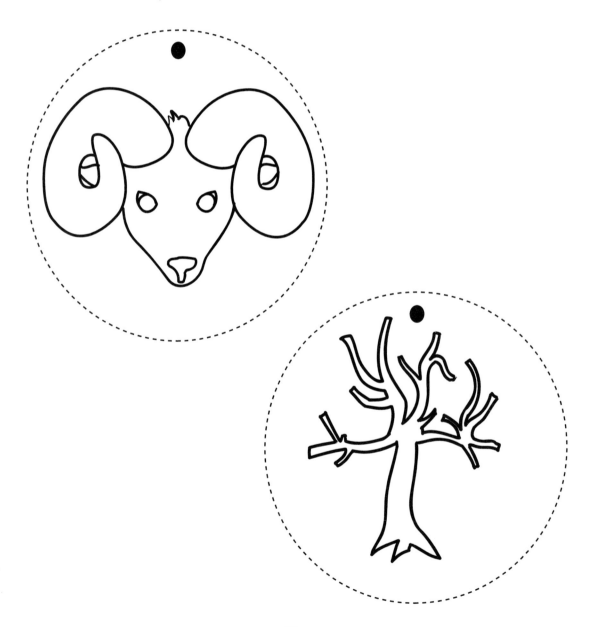

Isaac

My Favorite Things
♫ Genesis 22:1-18 ♫

Memory Verse

The Lord will provide.
~Genesis 22:14

What You Need

- duplicated page
- crayons

What to Do

Give each child a copy of this page. Ask them what God has provided for them. Discuss how He has provided good food to eat, a home to live in, a family who loves them, good friends, etc. Have them draw a picture in the frame of their favorite thing that God has provided for them.

What to Say

Abraham was ready to sacrifice his son Isaac to show God how much he loved Him. He wanted to be obedient to Him. Isaac was also willing to be obedient to God. This was how God knew they both loved Him and had faith in Him. By providing the ram in the thicket, God showed them how much He loved them and that He was willing to provide for them.

The Lord will provide. – Genesis 22:14

Isaac

Where Is It?
ꕥ Genesis 22:1-18 ꕥ

Memory Verse

The Lord will provide.
~Genesis 22:14

What You Need

• duplicated page
• crayons

What to Do

Give each child a duplicated page and instruct them to find the ram, campfire, ox and cart, tent, table and Isaac and circle them with a crayon.

What to Say

The ram was hidden in the weeds, yet God made Abraham and Isaac see it. He provided for them just in time. They rejoiced and worshipped and praised God for providing for them. How do you think Abraham and Isaac felt when they found the ram in the thicket? What has God given you to make you happy?

Miriam

Memory Verse

The Lord is my light and my salvation.
~Psalm 27:1

What You Need

• duplicated page
• crayons

What to Do

After reviewing the story, give each child a copy of this page. Tell them that Miriam begins with the letter M. Repeat the M sound together. Have them circle all of the items on the page that begin with the letter M. As they are doing this, ask, **Do you have any younger brothers or sisters? Do you help look out for them?**

What to Say

Miriam was so excited when she finally had a baby brother! She loved to help her mother take care of him. But something bad was happening. Pharaoh wanted all of the Hebrew baby boys killed. That meant Miriam's baby brother, Moses! She helped her mother hide Moses as long as they could. Soon, it became too hard to hide him. Miriam and her mother made a basket and placed him in the basket in the river. Miriam knew God would protect baby Moses.

Miriam

Baby Watching Binoculars
♪ Exodus 1:22-2:10 ♪

Memory Verse

The Lord is my light and my salvation.
~Psalm 27:1

What You Need

- toilet paper tubes
- glue
- paper clips
- tempera paints
- paint brushes
- paint smocks
- hole punch
- yarn

What to Do

Before class, gather two toilet paper tubes for each child. Show how to glue the tubes together and secure them with paper clips while they dry. Help the children into paint smocks (men's old shirts work well). Let each child paint their "binoculars" with tempera paints. After the binoculars have dried, go around the room and make a hole on each side of one end with a hole punch. Tie a length of yarn to each set of "binoculars" for a strap. Show how to use the "binoculars" to pretend you are Miriam watching for your baby brother. (Remind the children that Miriam did not have real binoculars to watch her brother, so she had to watch with her eyes.)

What to Say

Miriam had an important job to do. She was to watch her baby brother as he floated down the river. Her mother had put him there so the Pharaoh would not kill him. But Miriam saw the Pharaoh's own daughter find him. She didn't want any harm to come to him, but she would need help to care for him. That's when Miriam offered to have her mother help care for him. God protected the baby and made a way for his own mother to care for him.

22

Miriam

Berry Basket Baby
✿ Exodus 1:22-2:10 ✿

Memory Verse

Love never fails.
~1 Corinthians 13:8

What You Need

- page 24, duplicated
- plastic berry baskets
- scraps of yarn, lace and ribbons
- unshelled peanuts
- fine tip markers
- crayons
- safety scissors

What to Do

Give each child a plastic berry basket. Set out scraps of yarn, lace, ribbon, etc. for the children to weave in their baskets. Give each child an unshelled peanut. Allow them to put a face on one end of the peanut with a fine tip marker. Give each child a blanket from page 24 to color. Show how to wrap the peanut "baby" in the blanket and place it in the basket.

What to Say

When Miriam was a young girl, her mother had a baby boy. But Pharaoh wanted all of the Hebrew baby boys killed because he didn't like Hebrews. Miriam's mother didn't want her baby killed so she put him in a basket and floated him down the river. Miriam watched from the bushes as Pharaoh's own daughter found the basket. Why do you think Miriam watched the basket from the bushes? What do you think Miriam was thinking when the basket was found?

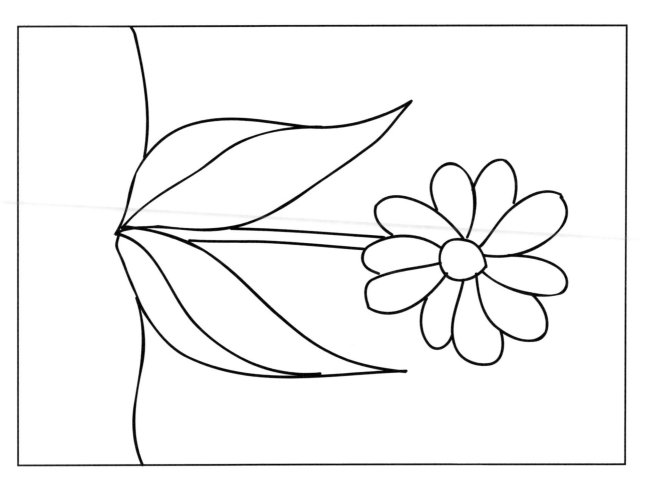

Miriam

See the Little Baby?
◦ Exodus 1:22-210 ◦

Memory Verse

The Lord is my light and my salvation.
~Psalm 27:1

What You Need

• page 26
• crayons

What to Do

Demonstrate the fun finger play below to help the children remember the story of how Moses was saved with the help of his big sister Miriam. Have the children perform it with you. Duplicate page 26 and repeat the poem as the children are coloring.

What to Say

Miriam had a new baby brother. She loved her baby brother very much, but he was in danger. Her mother had to hide him in a basket from Pharaoh, who wanted all the boy babies killed. It was Miriam's job to watch the basket that she and her mother had made to see where it went after they put it in the river. When the Pharaoh's own daughter found the baby, Miriam offered her mother to help care for the child. God protected this special baby boy.

See the Little Baby?

See the little baby boy   *Cup your hands around your eyes like binoculars.*

Floating in the reeds   *Make a floating motion with your right hand.*
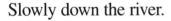

Slowly down the river.   *Continue the floating motion with your hand.*
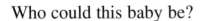

Who could this baby be?   *Put out both hands, palms up as if asking a question.*

For this is baby Moses.   *Cradle your arms.*

God's promises he'll share.   *Point up to heaven.*

When Pharaoh's daughter finds him   *Cup both hands together, palms up.*

Miriam and her mother help with his care.   *Cradle your arms.*

The Lord is my light and my salvation.
Psalm 27:1

Miriam

Love Never Fails
❧ Exodus 1:22–2:10 ❧

Memory Verse

Love never fails.
~1 Corinthians 13:8

What You Need

• page 28, duplicated
• crayons or markers
• paper grocery bags
• stapler
• masking tape
• newspapers

What to Do

Divide the class into teams of three to five children. Use the heart pattern on page 28 to cut out as many hearts as you have teams. Color each heart differently. Against a wall, set up as many grocery bags as you have teams and staple a different heart on each bag. Fold over the tops of the bags so they stay open. Place a piece of masking tape on the floor approximately three feet in front of the bags. Wad up several pieces of newspapers for balls and place behind the masking tape lines. Have each team stand behind the line facing their team's grocery bag. The first child in line should try to throw a newspaper wad into the grocery bag. With each throw, they are to say one of the words to the memory verse: "Love never fails." If they get the first one in as they say "Love," they are to try another while saying the word "never," and then "fails" with the third. If they miss, they are to try again until they have said all three words to the verse while throwing a paper ball. The first team to have all members make three baskets while saying the Scripture wins the game.

What to Say

Miriam loved God and her baby brother. She knew that God loved her and her brother, too. Because of God's love for them, she knew He would protect them. Love is very powerful. It can conquer even the worst of enemies.

Miriam

Find the Baby
♫ Exodus 1:22–2:10 ♫

Memory Verse

Love never fails.
~1 Corinthians 13:8

What You Need

- pattern below
- card stock
- page 30
- crayons

What to Do

Before class, use the outline below as a pattern to cut out a baby for each child from card stock. Copy page 30 for each child. Have the children color the river scene. Then show how to place the card stock baby underneath the picture. Say, "Miriam and her mother hid baby Moses in the water near the river's edge. Let's see if we can find him." Have the children rub a crayon over the area where the baby is underneath. Baby Moses will appear.

What to Say

Miriam had an important job to do. She was to watch to see what happened to her baby brother after they placed his basket in the river. She trusted that God would help keep him safe. She loved her baby brother and didn't want any harm to come to him. As she watched, Pharaoh's daughter found the baby. This was Miriam's chance! She offered to have her mother help care for the baby. God made a way for the baby to live and have his own mother help care for him.

29

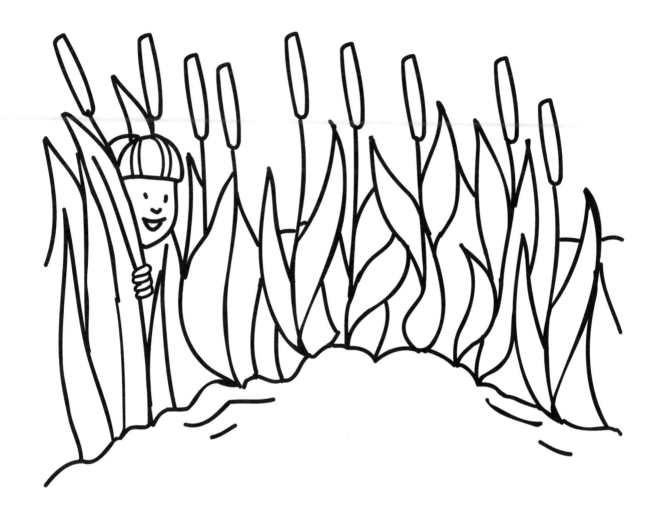

Samuel

S...S...Samuel
♪1 Samuel 2:18-19; 3:1-21♫

Memory Verse

The Lord looks at the heart.

~1 Samuel 16:7

What You Need

• duplicated page
• crayons

What to Do

After reviewing the story, give each child a duplicate of this page. Tell them that Samuel begins with the letter S. Repeat the S sound together. Have them circle the items on the page that begin with the letter S.

What to Say

As a baby, Samuel's life was given over to God by his mother. As a young boy, Samuel went to live at the temple with the priest, Eli. His heart was committed to the Lord even though he hadn't learned very much about Him yet. God knew that this young boy's heart was willing to serve Him. That's why He chose Samuel as one of His servants.

Samuel

A Robe for Samuel
♪ 1 Samuel 2:18-19; 3:1-21 ♫

Memory Verse

Each year his mother made him a little robe.
~1 Samuel 2:19

What You Need

• duplicated page
• glue
• fabric scraps
• safety scissors

What to Do

Give each child a copy of the Samuel doll and robe. Let them decorate the robe by gluing fabric scraps to it, just as Samuel's mother made him a special robe each year. Show how to cut out the paper doll and glue on his new robe.

What to Say

Both Samuel and his mother wanted to obey the Lord. Hannah loved her son, Samuel, very much and wanted to let him know that. Making him a new robe each year was one way she could show him that she loved him. How do you think Samuel felt each year when he received his new robe? What do you think his new robe looked like?

Samuel

I Listen with My Ears
♪ 1 Samuel 2:18-19; 3:1-21 ♫

Memory Verse

Then Samuel said, "Speak, for your servant is listening."

~1 Samuel 3:10

What You Need

- page 34
- play clay
- crayons

What to Do

Give each child a copy of page 34. Have them lay the page in front of them. With play clay, show how to form the missing ears. Encourage the students to enhance the other features of the face with clay, too. They may color the illustration to take home.

What to Say

When Samuel first came to live with Eli, he knew very little about God. He did know that he wanted to serve Him, though. When the Lord spoke to Samuel, he was willing to listen to Him and obey whatever it was the Lord asked of him. It was Samuel's willingness to listen and obey that made him a great servant of God.

Then Samuel said, "Speak, for your servant is listening."
1 Samuel 3:10

Samuel

Make a Promise Keeper
♪ 1 Samuel 2:18-19; 3:1-21 ♫

Memory Verse

Then Samuel said, "Speak, for your servant is listening."
~1 Samuel 3:10

What You Need

- pages 35 and 36
- markers
- glue
- glitter
- paper plates
- staplers
- safety scissors

What to Do

Give each child a copy of the stars on page 36 and a Promise Keeper label from below. Let them decorate the stars with markers, glue and glitter. While the children work on the stars, cut paper plates in half and staple a half onto a whole plate to make a pocket. Make one pocket plate for each child. Have them cut out and glue the Promise Keeper tag on the outside of the pouch. When the stars are dry, they should cut them out. Explain to the children that every time they make a promise and keep it, they should put one of their decorated stars in the Promise Keeper. Find out how many stars the children have collected the next time you meet together.

What to Say

Samuel was a very young boy when he went to live with the priest, Eli. Before he really knew who the Lord was, the Lord began speaking to him. Even at his young age, he knew that he must listen to the Lord and do what He said.

Promise Keeper

Samuel

What's That Sound?
♫ 1 Samuel 2:18-19; 3:1-21 ♫

Memory Verse

The Lord looks at the heart.

~1 Samuel 16:7

What You Need

• cassette tape
• tape player

What to Do

Before class, tape record several familiar sounds, such as a dog barking, a doorbell, a horn honking, a door closing, a telephone, etc. Explain to the students that you will be playing a listening game. Have the children lay on the floor. Tell them to listen to the sounds carefully. When they hear the designated sound that you choose, they are to sit up and say, "Samuel is listening!" Play several times, using many different sounds.

What to Say

When God saw Samuel, He didn't notice how young he was. What God saw was a young man who was willing to listen to God and obey Him. Samuel was eager to hear about God and learn about Him. He wanted to spend his life serving God.

Samuel

Your Servant Is Listening
♪ 1 Samuel 2:18-19; 3:1-21 ♪

Memory Verse

Then Samuel said, "Speak, for your servant is listening."

~1 Samuel 3:10

What You Need

- duplicated page
- safety scissors
- crayons
- tape

What to Do

Duplicate two megaphones from below for each child. Let them cut out and decorate them. Show how to tape them together at the tabs. Have the children sit in a circle while quietly holding their megaphones. Tell them that it is very important for everyone to remain quiet during this game. Choose one child to be It. It should sit in the center of the circle with his or her eyes covered. The teacher or leader should then walk around the outside of the circle and tap a child on the head. That child should say "Samuel, Samuel!" through the megaphone while disguising his or her voice. It should then try to figure out who called him or her and reply, "Speak, (child's name), for your servant is listening." If It guesses correctly, then the person who called out becomes It.

What to Say

When Samuel was a young boy, he went to live with the priest, Eli. One night he heard a voice calling him. He heard the voice three different times before he and Eli realized that it was the Lord calling Samuel. Once he realized it was the Lord, he was ready and willing to hear whatever it was the Lord needed to say to him. Whose voice was it that Samuel heard calling his name?

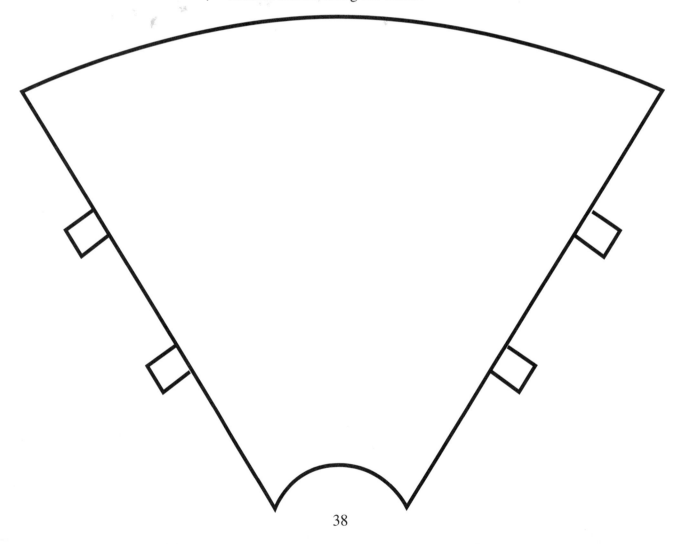

The Widow's Sons

Mystery of the Missing Jar
2 Kings 4:1-7

Memory Verse

May the God of hope fill you with all joy and peace as you trust in him.
~Romans 15:13

What You Need

• jar

What to Do

Hide the jar, then gather the children in a circle. Explain that you are going on a jar hunt. Give the students clues one at a time as to where the jar is hidden. It is up to them to figure out where that might be. The child who guesses where the jar is gets to whisper to you the next hiding place.

What to Say

All of the widow's money had run out and she had to pay her debts. If she did not come up with the money soon, she would have to turn her sons over to her debtors as slaves. But God had another plan. The prophet Elisha instructed her sons to find as many empty jars as they could and fill them with the oil from her own jar. God miraculously stretched her supply of oil to fill enough jars to pay off all her debts and give her enough money to live on. God cares for each one of us and supplies for all our needs in ways that we might never imagine.

The Widow's Sons

Jars of Hope
🎵 2 Kings 4:1-7 🎵

Memory Verse

May the God of hope fill you with all joy and peace as you trust in him.
~Romans 15:13

What You Need

- pages 40 and 41
- empty jars
- crayons
- safety scissors
- tape

What to Do

Before class, duplicate pages 40 and 41 for each child and remove the label on a jar for each child. Have the children color and cut out the "Hope" label on page 40. When the labels are complete, show how to put them inside the jar so that the decorated side is visible and secure with tape. Tell the students that they can fill the jars with the praise coupons (have them cut them apart from page 41). Explain that they should put one inside their jars each time God answers a prayer.

What to Say

The widow knew that Elisha could help her and her sons. She trusted God to supply their needs and had faith that Elisha would help. Her sons obeyed what their mother and Elisha asked them to do and God blessed them. When we trust and obey, we have the hope that only God can give. Do we always trust God for the things we need? What kinds of things do you pray to God for?

HOPE

May the God of hope fill you with all joy and peace as you trust in Him.

Romans 15:13

Praise Coupon	Praise Coupon
Praise Coupon	Praise Coupon
Praise Coupon	Praise Coupon
Praise Coupon	Praise Coupon

The Widow's Sons

Memory Verse

May the God of hope fill you with all joy and peace as you trust in him.
~Romans 15:13

What You Need

• duplicated page
• crayons

What to Do

Give each child a copy of the jars below. Help the children find and circle the two jars that are the same.

What to Say

The widow had faith that God could help her. She knew that Elisha was one of God's servants and would be able to tell her what to do. He told her to find as many jars as she could fill with oil. She gathered her sons and told them they must find as many jars as possible. They trusted that God would supply the oil they needed to fill the jars. God performed a miracle that day by filling all those jars!

The Widow's Sons

Jar Full of Miracles
⟡ 2 Kings 4:1-7 ⟡

Memory Verse

May the God of hope fill you with all joy and peace as you trust in him.
~Romans 15:13

What You Need

- duplicated page
- crayons

What to Do

Give each child a copy of this page. Count 1-20 aloud together. Instruct the children to connect the dots, starting with 1 and ending with 20. As they are doing this, tell them that they will be drawing a picture of what the widow's sons were told to collect.

What to Say

The widow's husband had died and the widow had no money to pay her debts. The people to whom she owed money were going to take away her sons and use them as slaves. The widow decided to pray and ask God what to do. She knew Elisha was a man of God. He told her to gather as many jars as she could, that her tiny bit of oil would fill them all and she could pay off her debts. She told her sons to find as many jars as they could. She and her sons were faithful to follow God's instructions. He was faithful to perform the miracle.

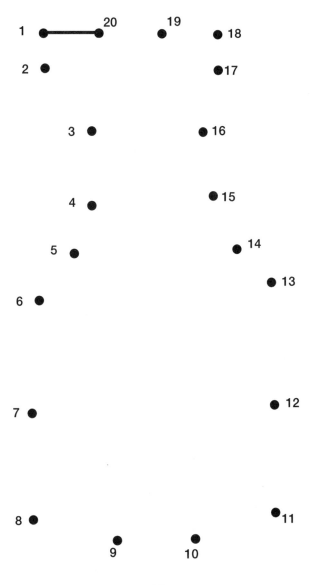

The Widow's Sons

Puppet Sons
2 Kings 4:1-7

Memory Verse

May the God of hope fill you with all joy and peace as you trust in him.
~Romans 15:13

What You Need

- duplicated page
- crayons
- paper lunch sacks
- old newspapers
- string
- safety scissors
- glue sticks

What to Do

Distribute this page to each child. Have them color and cut out the two sets of eyes and two mouths. Give each child two paper sacks. Have them wad up old newspapers into softball-sized balls and place them in the sacks (one per sack). Go around and tie the sacks closed with string just under the newspaper balls. These are the sons' heads. Allow the students to glue the eyes and mouths on the sacks. Show how to put your hand in the opening and act out the story.

What to Say

The widow and her sons were out of money and out of food. The widow didn't know what to do. Her sons would be sold as slaves if she couldn't pay her debts. The woman and her family had always trusted in the Lord and knew that He would help her. She went to the prophet Elisha for help. He told her to have her sons gather as many jars as possible and fill them with oil. They did as they were told. God miraculously multiplied their oil. They had enough to sell to pay their debts.

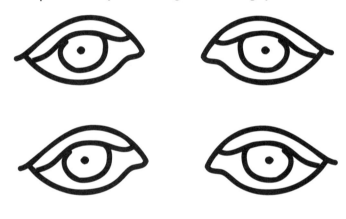

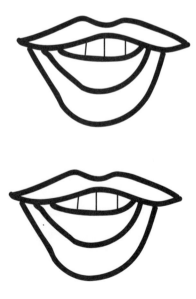

Naaman's Servant Girl

Walk in the Way of the Lord
♪ 2 Kings 5:1-16 ♫

Memory Verse

Blessed are all who fear the Lord, who walk in his ways.

~Psalm 128:1

What You Need

• obstacle course
• stopwatch

What to Do

Before class, set up a simple obstacle course in your classroom. Set out obstacles such as chairs to walk around, boxes to climb over, under or through, etc. After you tell the story of Naaman and the servant girl, tell the students that you are going to help Naaman find his way to Elisha to be healed. Time the children going through the obstacle course.

What to Say

Naaman had to have faith that the prophet Elisha, who lived in a far away country, could help him. Naaman's servant girl said that Elisha was a prophet from the true God. Naaman wasn't sure who this God was that his servant girl was telling him about. But he knew that if He could heal him, then He must be the one true God. He did!

Naaman's Servant Girl

Little Servant Girl
ᔫ 2 Kings 5:1-16 ᔫ

Memory Verse

Commit your way to the Lord.

~Psalm 37:5

What You Need

• duplicated page

What to Do

Demonstrate the finger play below for the children then have them do it with you. Give each child a copy of this page to take home.

What to Say

Naaman's little servant girl committed her life to serving the Lord. Because of her faith, she was not afraid to tell Naaman of Elisha and the Lord's power to heal him.

I'm a little servant girl	*Point to yourself.*
Who wants to do God's will.	*Point to heaven.*
My master is a powerful man,	*Crook your arm to show your muscle.*
But he is very, very ill.	*Put the back of your hand to your forehead.*
I know the Lord can heal him;	*Point to heaven.*
I want to let him know.	*Hold out both hands, palms up.*
He must find the prophet Elisha.	*Put your hand up to your eyebrows.*
To my homeland he must go.	*Point a finger away with your arm straight out.*
Elisha gives instruction,	*Shake your finger.*
"Wash seven times, no more,	*Hold up seven fingers.*
In the Jordan River's water.	*Make a flowing motion with your hands.*
You'll be better than before!"	*Hold your hands up in praise to God.*

Naaman's Servant Girl

Naaman's Obedience Walk
~ 2 Kings 5:1-16 ~

Memory Verse

Blessed are all who fear the Lord, who walk in his ways.

~Psalm 128:1

What You Need

- tape
- duplicated page
- seven crayons

What to Do

Place tape on the floor to indicate a start line and a finish line. Duplicate seven of the soap pattern below. Cut them out and color each one a different color; give each child one. If you have more than seven children, make as many as you need but use only seven different colors. If you have fewer than seven children, the children may have more than one card, but make sure each child has the same number of cards. Have the children line up at one end of the room. Remind them that Naaman had to obey God and wash in the Jordan River seven times to be healed of his disease. The leader should call out a color and something for the person who is holding that color to do, such as hop three times forward. Continue doing this, alternating colors until one person reaches the finish line.

What to Say

Even though Naaman didn't understand why Elisha told him to wash in the Jordan River, he did as he was told. He knew that the water in that river wouldn't cure him, but the power of God would. After Naaman was healed, he knew that the God Elisha worshipped was the only true God.

Naaman's Servant Girl

Obey the Lord
ᔆ 2 Kings 5:1-16 ᔆ

Memory Verse

Blessed are all who fear the Lord, who walk in his ways.

~Psalm 128:1

What You Need

• duplicated page
• crayons, blue and yellow

What to Do

Give each child a copy of this page. Have them color blue the shapes that have a dot and yellow those without a dot. When the picture is finished, it will say what we are to do when God asks us to do something.

What to Say

The little slave girl who worked for Naaman loved and feared the Lord. She knew that God could heal Naaman if he would obey Him. What are we to do when we know God wants us to do something?

David the Shepherd Boy

D...D...David
♪ 1 Samuel 17:34-37 ♫

Memory Verse

Watch, stand fast in faith, be brave, be strong.

~1 Corinthians 16:13

What You Need

• duplicated page
• crayons

What to Do

After reviewing the story, give each child a duplicate of this page. Tell them that David begins with the letter D. Say the D sound together. Ask them to circle all of the items on the page that start with the letter D.

What to Say

David learned at a very early age to trust in the Lord. As a young shepherd boy, he was constantly protecting his sheep and himself from dangerous animals. David knew that the Lord would take care of him. What do you do when you are afraid? When was a time you had to be brave?

David the Shepherd Boy

David Protects His Sheep
♪ 1 Samuel 17:34-37 ♫

Memory Verse

Trust in the Lord and do good.

~Psalm 37:3

What You Need

- duplicate patterns (below)
- yellow and orange curling ribbon
- scissors
- dessert-size paper plates
- safety scissors
- glue
- crayons

What to Do

Before class, cut enough 12" pieces of curling ribbon so that each child will have at least 8-10 pieces. Curl the ribbon. Give each child a paper plate and have them color and cut out the lion's face features, then glue them onto the center of the plate. Have them glue pieces of curling ribbon to the edges of the plate for the mane.

What to Say

David was a shepherd boy. His job was to watch over his father's sheep. He had to make sure they had food and water and were out of danger. It was a big job for such a young boy! David loved and trusted God and knew that He would help him in everything. When a lion came and tried to carry off one of his sheep, David chased it and struck it down. He knew that God was protecting him then and that God would always protect him. Have you ever seen a lion at the zoo? Do you think David could have saved the sheep from the lion without God's help and protection?

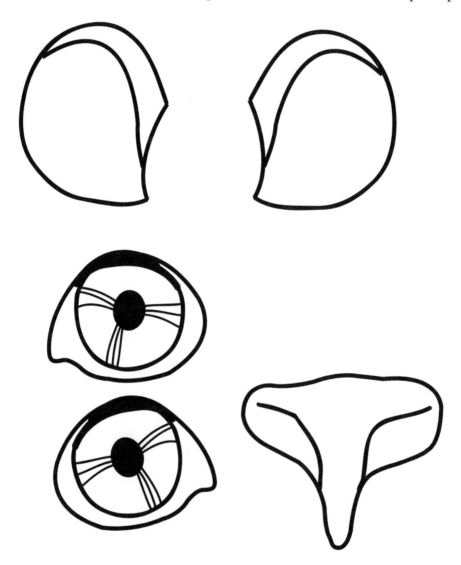

50

David the Shepherd Boy

Chain of Protection
𝒮 1 Samuel 17:34-37 𝒞

Memory Verse

Watch, stand fast in faith, be brave, be strong.

~1 Corinthians 16:13

What You Need

- page 52
- construction paper
- glue sticks
- safety scissors

What to Do

Before class, copy the chain strips on page 52 for each child and cut several 1" x 6" strips of construction paper. Read the words on the chain strips to the class and tell them that they are going to make a long chain that they will put around them for protection. Show how to cut apart and link the strips, then let the children work together to make a long chain from the Scripture strips and the plain construction paper. When the chain is all done, make a large circle on the floor with it. Have the children sit inside the circle. Discuss how David had faith that God would protect him, even against wild animals.

What to Say

David was just a young boy, but he had an important job to do. He had to protect his sheep. He had to make sure they had enough food and water. He even had to protect them from other wild animals such as lions and bears. Knowing that God would help protect him, David had the courage to fight off the wild animals while protecting his flock. He knew that God loved him and would be faithful to protect him while he tended his sheep. We can have faith that God will protect us, too. (Ask the children from what kinds of things God can protect them.)

WATCH,

STAND FAST

IN FAITH,

BE BRAVE,

BE STRONG. 1 Corinthians 16:13

David the Shepherd Boy

Veggie Creatures
♪ 1 Samuel 17:34-37 ♫

Memory Verse

Watch, stand fast in faith, be brave, be strong.

~1 Corinthians 16:13

What You Need

• bowls
• raw vegetables
• toothpicks

What to Do

Set out bowls of several kinds of fresh, raw vegetables such as broccoli, cauliflower, carrot slices, mushrooms, celery pieces, etc. Using toothpicks, show how to put together the veggie pieces to look like different animals. Make a cauliflower sheep using a piece of cauliflower for the body and a mushroom for the head and celery sticks for the legs.

What to Say

David cared for every one of his sheep. He trusted God to help him keep them safe from harm. Through his faith he was brave and strong against any enemy. God cares for us just as the shepherd boy, David, cared for his sheep. Having faith in God as our shepherd, we can also be brave and strong in any circumstance.

David the Shepherd Boy

We Are God's Sheep
♪ 1 Samuel 17:34-37 ♫

Memory Verse

Trust in the Lord and do good.

~Psalm 37:3

What You Need

• play clay (see recipe)
• duplicated page
• waxed paper
• tape

What to Do

Before class, make a batch of play clay (see recipe below). Do not add color to it. Make a copy of the pasture scene below for each child. Tape one on the table in front of each child with a piece of waxed paper over it. Using the play clay, show the children how to make a sheep: Roll one ball, approximately 2" in diameter. Roll another ball about 1" in diameter and place it on the larger ball, off center, to be the sheep's head. Make four legs and put on the body. Place your sheep in the pasture scene.

What to Say

When David was a young boy, he took care of his family's sheep. He made sure they had enough to eat and drink and that they were safe. We are like God's sheep. He watches over us and protects us, just as David did with his sheep, making sure that all are safe. What kinds of things do you think David had to do to take care of his sheep? Are we more important to God than sheep? Does God take good care of us?

Play Clay:

Mix together in a saucepan 2 cups flour, 4 teaspoons cream of tartar, 1 cup salt, 2 cups water and 2 tablespoons vegetable oil. Cook and stir over medium heat about 3-5 minutes (it will look like a globby mess). When the mixture is about the consistency of stiff mashed potatoes and has formed a ball in the center of the pot, turn it out and knead it on a lightly floured surface. Store in an airtight container.

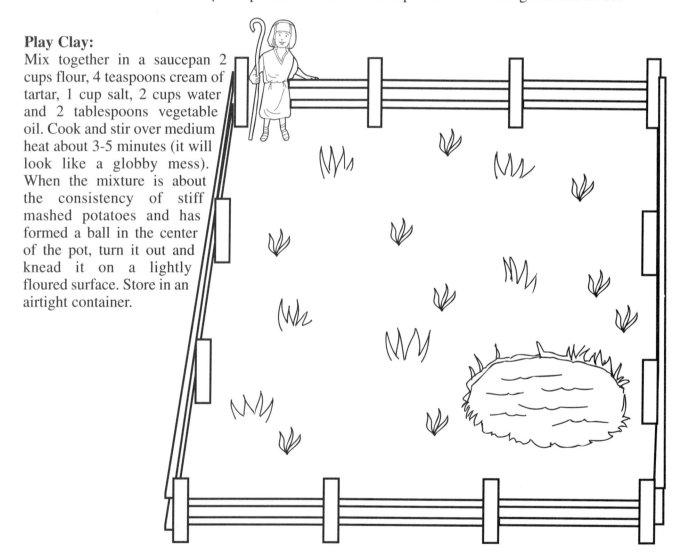

David and Goliath

The Lord's Battle
☞ 1 Samuel 17:4-51 ☜

Memory Verse

For the battle is the Lord's.

~1 Samuel 17:47

What You Need

- pages 55 and 56
- crayons
- safety scissors
- glue sticks
- paper plates
- construction paper
- tape

What to Do

Duplicate this page and the shield on page 56 for each child. Have the children draw something they are afraid of in the shield. Then have them cut out the shield and glue it onto a paper plate with a glue stick. Read the words on the bottom of the page, then instruct the children to cut them out and glue them under the shield. On the back side of each child's plate, tape a 1" x 6" strip of construction paper as a strap for them to hold the shield.

What to Say

Even though David was just a young man, he knew that the giant Goliath must not be allowed to torment God's people any longer with his threats of war. He knew God was on his side. David was part of God's army. God is more powerful than any person on earth. David knew that if he had faith in God that he would be able to defeat Goliath. (Talk about fears. Ask if anyone thinks David might have been afraid when he faced Goliath.) How can we overcome our fears?

For the battle is the Lord's.

1 Samuel 17:47

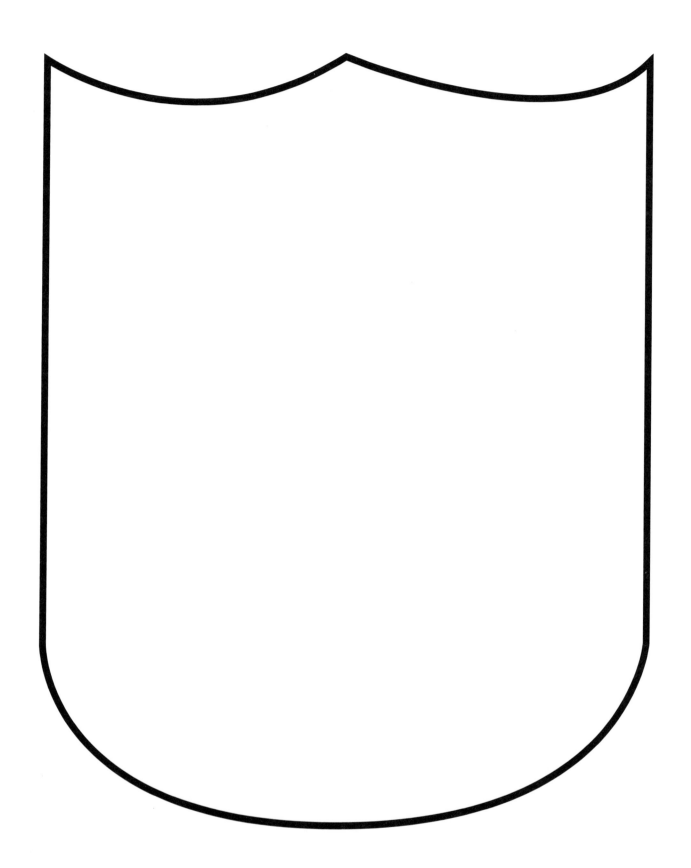

David and Goliath

Memory Verse

For the battle is the Lord's.

~1 Samuel 17:47

What You Need

• duplicated page
• crayons

What to Do

Give each child a copy of this page. Count the five stones with them, then allow them to trace the numbers and color the illustration.

What to Say

David was a young shepherd boy who stayed at home and helped his father tend their sheep while his older brothers went off to battle. While visiting his brothers, David was called by God to defeat the army's greatest enemy, Goliath. David was able to do this by trusting in God and relying on God's power.

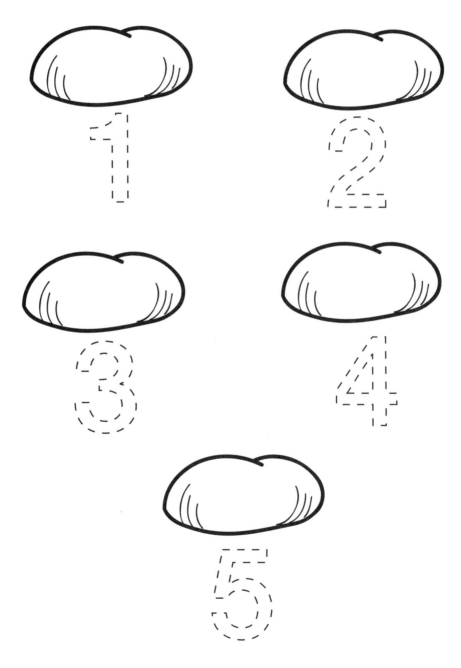

David and Goliath

Five Stones of Faith
♪ 1 Samuel 17:4-51 ♫

Memory Verse

Trust in the Lord and do good.

~Psalm 37:3

What You Need

- smooth stones
- page 59
- crayons
- safety scissors
- cotton swabs
- glue

What to Do

Gather smooth stones for the children. (If the weather permits, let the children find their own stones.) Copy the stars and happy faces on page 59 for the children to cut out. Let the students color the stars and happy faces, then cut them out. Show how to use a cotton swab to "paint" white glue on the rocks and place the colored pictures on them.

What to Say

Because David trusted God and had faith in Him, he knew he could defeat Goliath. With faith, we can "Trust in the Lord and do good" (Psalm 37:3). God gave David the courage to face Goliath! Do you know how he fought Goliath? How many stones did it take to win? Take home your Stone of Courage to remind you that if you have faith in God, you are a winner, too.

David and Goliath

Memory Verse

Trust in the Lord and do good.

~Psalm 37:3

What You Need

- pages 60 and 61
- old magazines
- safety scissors
- 11" x 17" construction paper
- glue sticks

What to Do

Photocopy the Scripture at the bottom of this page and the heart on page 61 for each child. Read the Scripture to the students and have them repeat it with you. From old magazines, have the children cut out pictures of anything that God provides. They can cut out pictures of families, plants, trees, food, flowers, friends, etc. Give each child a sheet of 11" x 17" construction paper and have the students cut out and glue on the heart. Show how to cut out the letter boxes from the bottom of this page and attach them below the heart with a glue stick (they can look at the heart for help). Then allow them to arrange and glue on the pictures they have cut out.

What to Say

David knew that God provided everything good for His people. He knew that if he trusted God, he could do good. When Goliath challenged Saul's army, David knew that if he trusted in God, he could defeat the giant. Even today, God provides all good things for us. When we trust in Him, we can do good, just like David.

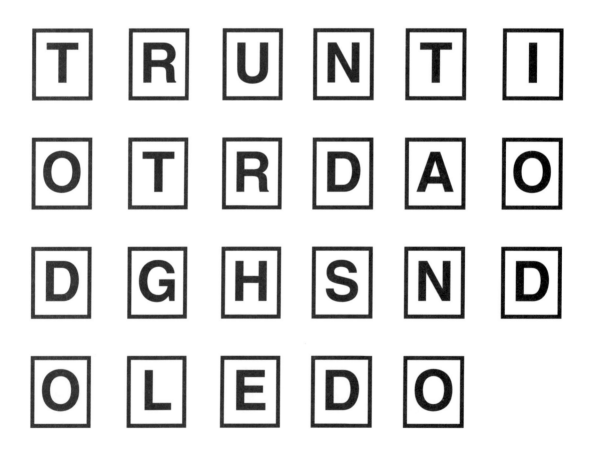

Trust in the Lord and do good.

Psalm 37:3

David and Goliath

Memory Verse

Trust in the Lord and do good.

~Psalm 37:3

What You Need

• duplicated page
• crayons
• rubber bands
• glue

What to Do

Give each child a copy of this page. Have the children color the picture and glue a small rubber band in David's hand to represent the sling shot.

What to Say

When David heard Goliath speaking against God and challenging people to fight him, he knew what he had to do. David knew that God could keep him safe and help him defeat the giant. David trusted and obeyed God and because of that, God protected him and he was able to do mighty things. Do you think David was afraid? What do you think his brothers were thinking?

Jesus

J...J...Jesus
♪ Luke 2:41-52 ♪

Memory Verse

Jesus grew in wisdom and stature.

~Luke 2:52

What You Need

• duplicated page
• crayons

What to Do

After reviewing the story, give each child a duplicate of this page. Tell the students that Jesus' name begins with the letter J. Repeat the J sound together. Have the children circle the items on the page that begin with the letter J.

What to Say

Jesus came to earth as a baby, just like all of us. While growing up He knew that His Father was God. He wanted to learn all He could about Him. We all love to listen to stories about our parents and grandparents — Jesus did too! That's why He stayed behind at the temple, to hear more about His Heavenly Father. What kinds of things do you like to learn about?

Jesus

Blow Painting Maze
~Luke 2:41-52~

Memory Verse

Then they began looking for him.

~Luke 2:44

What You Need

• duplicated page
• plastic drinking straws
• tempera paint
• paint smocks

What to Do

Give each child a maze and a clean straw. You will want to cover each child's clothes with a smock — men's old shirts work well. Place a drop of tempera paint on the area marked "start" on each page. Have the children blow the paint through straws along the maze to help Mary and Joseph find Jesus. Add more paint when necessary.

What to Say

Mary and Joseph were most likely feeling afraid when they realized that their son Jesus was not with them. They immediately turned around and began searching for Him. When they found Him back at the temple, He was surprised that they didn't think to look there first, since that was His Father's house.

FINISH

START

Jesus

Is That You, Jesus?
Luke 2:41-52

Memory Verse

Jesus grew in wisdom and stature.

~Luke 2:52

What You Need

- pattern below
- craft stick
- music cassette tape
- cassette player

What to Do

Cut out the boy Jesus figure below and glue it on a craft stick. Have the children sit in a circle with their hands in their laps. Choose a child to be It. Have It stand in the center of the circle and cover and close his or her eyes. Give a child sitting in the circle the Jesus figure. Tell that child that when you start the music, he or she should pass the figure to the next person and continue to do this until the music stops. During this whole time, It is to keep his or her eyes covered and closed. When the music stops It may uncover his or her eyes and try to figure out who is holding the Jesus figure. They are to say "Is that You, Jesus?" as they point to whom they believe has the figure. If they are wrong, the child they are pointing at just says no. If they are correct, the child with the figure stands up and says "And Jesus grew in wisdom and stature." The child who was holding the figure then becomes It and the game begins again.

What to Say

Even while Jesus was a young boy, He knew who His heavenly Father was. He wanted to know as much about Him as He could. He knew that the teachers at the temple could teach Him a lot. He didn't intend to worry His parents when He was missing. He continued to grow into a fine young man.

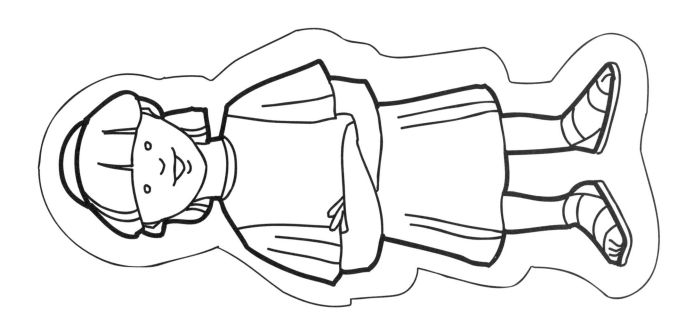

Jesus

Jesus Is Here—Can You Find Him?
♫ Luke 2:41-52 ♫

Memory Verse

Then they began looking for him.

~Luke 2:44

What You Need

• duplicated page
• crayons

What to Do

Distribute this page to each child. Read the coloring code to the children, noting where to use the different colors.

What to Say

Joseph and Mary and their children were starting their long journey home. They had walked all day and had covered quite a distance, but there was still a long way to go. It was just about evening when they realized that their son, Jesus, was not with them. They thought that He had been walking with some of their other relatives. They hurried back to Jerusalem to search for Him. They finally found Him in the temple, listening to the teachers and learning about God. Have you ever had to look for someone? How did you feel once you found him or her?

 = BLUE

▲ = YELLOW

● = BROWN

Jairus' Daughter

A Little Girl Is Healed
♪ Mark 5:21-24; 35-43 ♫

Memory Verse

"Little girl, I say to you, get up!"
~Mark 5:41

What You Need

- pages 67 and 68
- crayons
- safety scissors

What to Do

Duplicate this page and page 68 for each child. Have the children color the picture of Jairus' daughter and the eyes on the strips on the bottom of this page. Show how to cut slits in the picture and cut out the strips of eyes. Demonstrate how to slide the eyes through the slits so they change them from sleeping to awake.

What to Say

Jairus went to find Jesus because he had faith that He could heal his sick daughter. But when they returned to his home and found that she had already died, he was so sad! What could Jesus do now? Jesus has power even over death. He was able to make the little girl alive again! Jesus loves everyone, especially children.

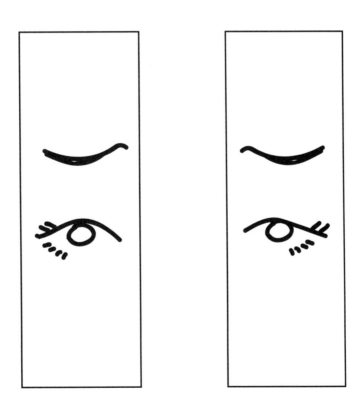

"Little girl, I say to you, get up!"
Mark 5:41

Jairus' Daughter

Circle the Differences
♪ Mark 5:21-24; 35-43 ♫

Memory Verse

"Little girl, I say to you, get up!"

~Mark 5:41

What You Need

• duplicated page
• crayons

What to Do

Give each child a copy of the two pictures below. Explain that there are four things different in the pictures. Have the students circle the differences.

What to Say

After Jesus healed the little girl, Jairus and his family were so amazed! They had been sad, but Jesus gave them a special gift — their little girl. Their daughter had been sick for so long. She was like a new girl!

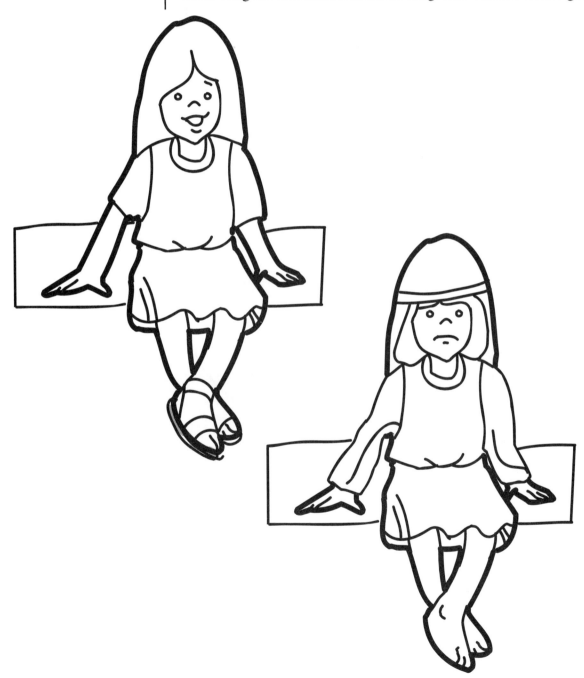

Jairus' Daughter

Memory Verse

"Don't be afraid, just believe."

~Mark 5:36

What You Need

- pattern below
- scissors
- glue
- craft stick

What to Do

Copy and cut out the two happy faces below and glue them together with a craft stick sandwiched between them to make a puppet. Gather the children in a seated circle. Choose one child to be It. Instruct the rest of the class to close their eyes so that they can't see anything. It should walk around the outside of the circle while holding the happy face puppet, and count to 10 aloud as he or she walks. When It gets to 10, he or she should stop and say, "Don't be afraid, just believe," then touch the child he or she is standing behind with the Happy Face Puppet. The child that is touched then chases It around the circle while It tries to get back to that child's spot. The child who was touched then becomes It and the game starts over.

What to Say

Jairus' daughter had been sick for a long time. Jairus was afraid she was going to die. He had heard that a man named Jesus could heal people. He went to find Him. But before they could get back to Jairus' house, the little girl had died. Jesus told them to not be afraid, just believe. The little girl was alive!

70

Jairus' Daughter

Memory Verse

"Don't be afraid, just believe."

~Mark 5:36

What You Need

• duplicated page
• large sheet of paper
• marker
• crayons

What to Do

Give each child a copy of this page. Print the words "Just Believe" on a large piece of paper and hang it up for the children to see. Read it to them and tell them that the words are hidden on the paper. They are to find the words and circle them. They can also color in all of the squares with letters that are not in the words.

What to Say

It had taken Jairus a while to find Jesus. He knew they had to hurry back if they were to help his daughter. It took longer than they thought and by the time they reached Jairus' house, it was too late. Jairus was so sad. But Jesus had other plans. He loved the little girl and Jairus very much and because of His love and great power, He was able to heal the little girl. If we have faith in God, He can do great miracles in our lives, too. He cares for us and takes care of us, just like He did for Jairus and his daughter.

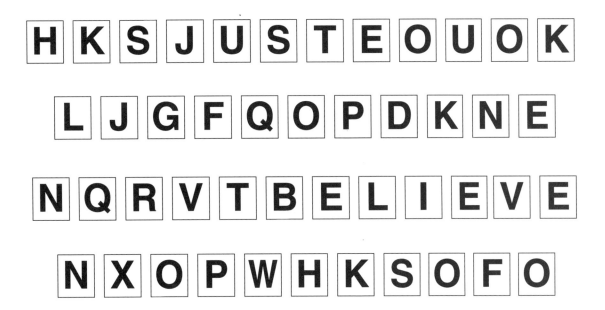

Jairus' Daughter

Rag Doll and Bed
∽ Mark 5:21-24; 35-43 ∾

Memory Verse

"Don't be afraid, just believe."

~Mark 5:36

What You Need

• 12" x 12" scraps of fabric
• cotton balls
• 3 rubber bands
• thin tip markers
• page 73
• tape

What to Do

Before class, copy the doll bed for each child. Have the children clump together 6-8 cotton balls into one ball. Let each child select a fabric scrap. Show how to find the center of the fabric scrap and put the cotton ball there. Help the children bring the fabric scrap all up around the cotton ball and secure a rubber band around it (this is the doll's head). Assist the students in gathering up a corner at each side of the head and putting a rubber band around these for arms. Allow them to use markers to draw a face on the doll. Give each child a copy of the bed to cut out. Help them make the doll bed by folding the sides down on the dotted lines. Show where to tape together the corners.

What to Say

Jairus' daughter had been sick for a long time. The only thing she could do was lay in bed. Before Jesus and her father could reach her, she died. But Jesus loved her very much. Because He is more powerful than death, He was able to heal her. She could finally get up out of her bed.

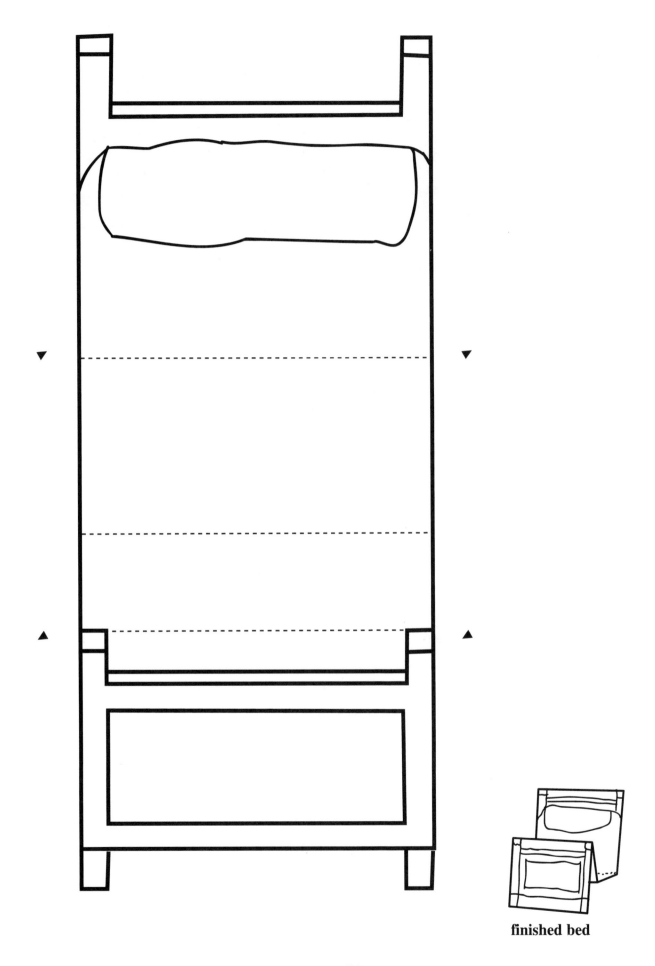

finished bed

Jairus' Daughter

Memory Verse

"Little girl, I say to you, get up!"
~Mark 5:41

What You Need

• page 75
• adhesive bandages
• crayons

What to Do

Duplicate the picture on page 75 for each child. Set out different sizes, shapes and colors of adhesive bandages. Have the children use the bandages to fill in the illustration of the little girl. They may also use crayons to decorate the pictures.

What to Say

Jairus didn't know where else to turn. His little girl had been sick for a long time. Nothing seemed to help her get better. He knew that if things didn't change, she would most likely die. Someone had told him about a great teacher named Jesus. He said that He was the Son of God. Surely He could help her. Jairus went to find Him, but while he was gone, his little girl died. When Jesus got to Jairus' house, He sent everyone away. He commanded the little girl to get up, and she did! Jesus had brought her back to life. Only His power was strong enough to conquer death. When you get hurt or don't feel well, do you sometimes put a bandage on your wound or take some medicine?

"Little girl, I say to you, get up!" Mark 5:41

Boy and His Lunch

To Share Is to Love
❧ John 6:5-14; 25-40 ❧

Memory Verse

Then Jesus declared, "I am the bread of life. He who comes to me will never go hungry."
~John 6:35

What You Need

- page 77
- crayons
- safety scissors
- tape
- goldfish crackers

What to Do

Duplicate the basket pattern on page 77 for each child. Let them color the basket and cut it out. Show how to fold it on the dotted lines and tape the letters together at the corners, then bring the two handle pieces together and tape them.

What to Say

No matter where Jesus went, people flocked around Him to hear His teaching. One day, He had been teaching for a long time. After a while, Jesus realized that the people must be getting hungry. There was no food around to give them. Then a little boy offered to share his small lunch with Jesus. Because Jesus loved everyone so much and wanted to care for them, He was able to turn that small lunch into enough food to feed everyone there and still have food leftover. Your baskets are empty right now. Unless someone shares with you, they will remain empty. Because the little boy was willing to share his lunch, Jesus was able to give everyone some food. (Have a child distribute goldfish crackers to each child, sharing with everyone.)

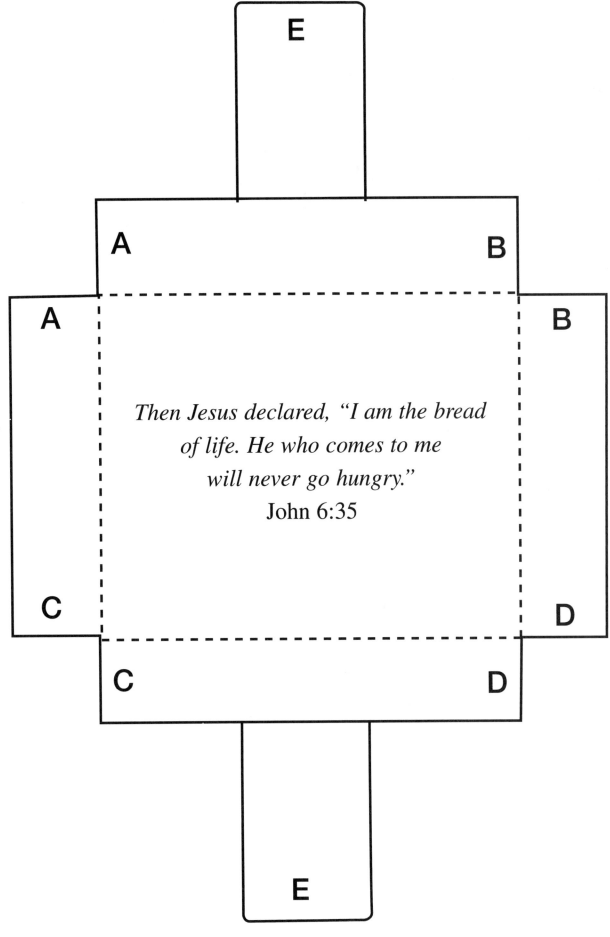

E

A B

A B

Then Jesus declared, "I am the bread of life. He who comes to me will never go hungry."
John 6:35

C D

C D

E

Boy and His Lunch

Memory Verse

Trust in the Lord with all your heart.

~Proverbs 3:5

What You Need

• duplicated page
• crayons

What to Do

Give each child a copy of this page. Count aloud together how many things are in each basket. Have the children trace the number under each basket.

What to Say

When the people saw Jesus and His disciples begin passing out the bread and the fish, most of them probably thought there wouldn't be enough. To their surprise, Jesus was able to feed everyone and still have food left over. If it wasn't for the willingness of the little boy to share with Jesus, no one would have had anything to eat. The boy's obedience and Jesus' power made it all possible. Would you think that five little loaves of bread and two fish could feed 5,000 people? How did Jesus feed so many people with so little food?

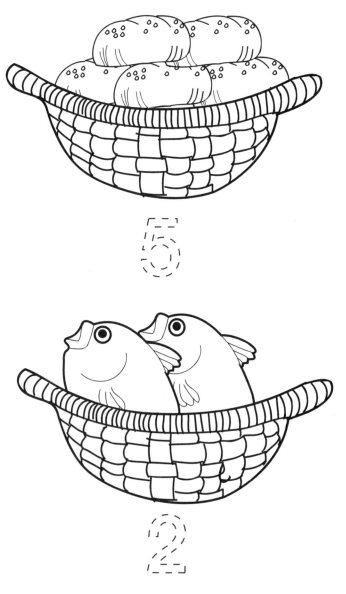

Boy and His Lunch

Fishy Concentration Game
John 6:5-14; 25-40

Memory Verse

Then Jesus declared, "I am the bread of life. He who comes to me will never go hungry."
~John 6:35

What You Need

• page 80, duplicated
• card stock
• crayons
• scissors

What to Do

Make two copies of page 80 on card stock for each child. Cut them apart. Give each child two sets of fish numbered 1 through 6. Let them decorate the numbered side of their fish cards with crayons, leaving the other side blank. To play the game, have the students turn the cards face down. They should use their memory to try to turn over two matching numbers at once. The game can be played alone or with a friend.

What to Say

There were 5,000 people present the day Jesus fed them with just two fish and five loaves of bread. Jesus knew that they were hungry. This was the perfect opportunity for Him to show His love and power by allowing a young boy to be part of His miracle. Because this boy was willing to share, Jesus was able to do a miraculous thing. What do you think would have happened if the little boy hadn't been willing to share his lunch?

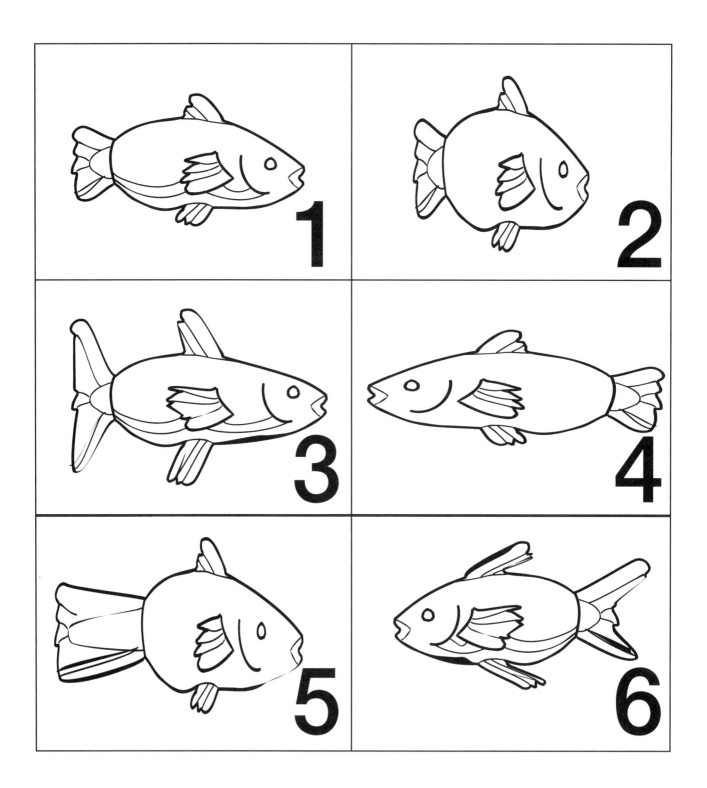

Boy and His Lunch

Loaf and Fish Mobile
ᔕ John 6:5-14; 25-40 ᔕ

Memory Verse

Then Jesus declared, "I am the bread of life. He who comes to me will never go hungry."
~John 6:35

What You Need

- page 82
- safety scissors
- crayons
- stapler
- newspaper
- string
- paper plates
- hole punch
- tape

What to Do

Before class, duplicate the loaves of bread and fish on page 82 so that each child has four fish and ten loaves of bread. Cut string into seven 14" lengths per child. Cut the paper plates in half. Instruct the students to color their fish and loaves. Staple two of each item together, leaving open one end. Show the children how to stuff each object with newspaper and staple them shut. Show how to tape a length of string to each object. Demonstrate how to punch seven holes on the curved edge of a plate half, spacing evenly. Help the students tie the objects through the holes in this order: loaf, loaf, fish, loaf, fish, loaf, loaf. Have them punch two more holes along the straight edge, 2" or 3" from each edge. Tie a piece of yarn in each mobile to make a hanger.

What to Say

Sharing isn't always an easy thing to do. Jesus asked the young boy to give up his lunch so that it could be shared with thousands of people. The boy was probably hungry himself, but was willing to share. Because of his act, Jesus was able to miraculously feed everyone in that crowd and still have leftovers. When we are unselfish, great things can happen through small acts.

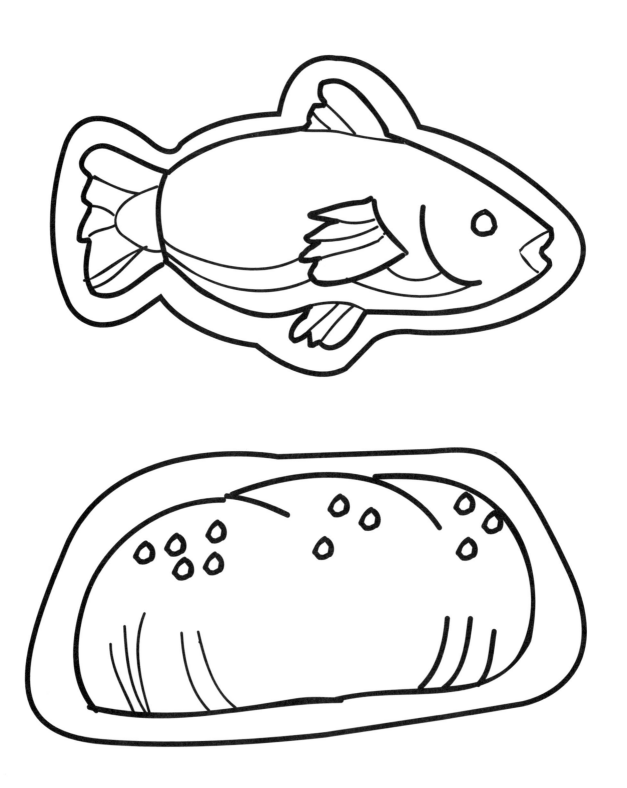

Boy and His Lunch

Bread of Life
𝄞 John 6:5-14; 25-40 𝄞

Memory Verse

Then Jesus declared, "I am the bread of life. He who comes to me will never go hungry."
~John 6:35

What You Need

- 11" x 17" construction paper
- tape
- duplicated page
- safety scissors
- glue

What to Do

Before class, duplicate this page and cut several strips of colored construction paper into 1" x 11" strips. Give each child a piece of 11" x 17" construction that has approximately six or seven horizontal slits, leaving at least a $1^1/2$" edge on each side. Let the children weave the pre-cut strips through the slits in the paper, taping down the edges. Allow them to cut out and glue the fish and bread on the place mats. During your snack time, use the place mats and discuss how Jesus made sure that everyone had enough to eat.

What to Say

Jesus looked around at the crowd who had come to hear Him teach. He knew that they were getting hungry, but what was He to do? He had no food of His own to share. Then Jesus' friends pointed out a little boy who had brought his own lunch. Jesus asked if he would let Him share it with all of the hungry people there. The little boy was willing to share what he had. Everyone was fed. Our place mats are a reminder of the little boy's obedience and the power of Jesus. As we eat, we can remember who gives us all good things.

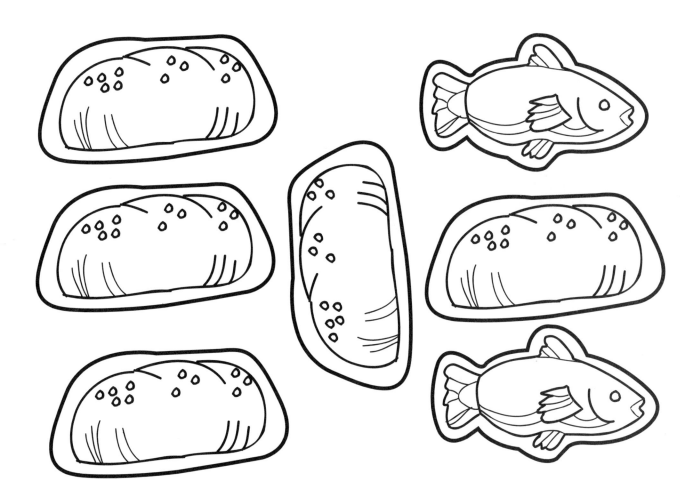

Boy and His Lunch

Memory Verse

Trust in the Lord with all your heart.

~Proverbs 3:5

What You Need

- page 85
- lunch-size paper sacks
- crayons
- safety scissors
- glue sticks
- snack

What to Do

Duplicate page 85 for each child. Give each child a paper sack. Let the children color and decorate the items on the duplicated page and cut them out. Show how to glue them on the lunch sack. Encourage the children to place their snacks inside the bag.

What to Say

Everywhere Jesus looked, there were people. There were over 5,000 people listening to Him that day. Jesus loved every one of the people there. It was getting late and they were all getting hungry. Jesus was worried about the people and knew He had to feed them, but how? His friends told Him that one little boy had brought his lunch. It was just a small lunch, but he was willing to share it. Because Jesus cared for everyone so much, He was able to take the small lunch that the little boy shared and feed all of the people there. There was even food left over when they were done.

Trust in the Lord

Boy and His Lunch

What's for Lunch?

John 6:5-14; 25-40

Memory Verse

"I am the bread of life."

~John 6:35

What You Need

• page 87
• crayons

What to Do

Copy page 87 for each child. Discuss each of the items in the illustration. Have the children circle the items that they might put in their lunch.

What to Say

The little boy had been listening to Jesus teach all day and was probably getting very hungry. His mother had packed him a lunch of two fish and five little loaves of bread. But there were many people listening to Jesus and few had food. The boy asked if he could give his lunch to Jesus so that it could be shared with everyone there. There were so many people! How could this little lunch help? Jesus took the lunch and through His great power it fed everyone. What are some of your favorite things to eat for lunch? Would you give up your lunch and share it with others like the little boy in the story did?

Timothy

Memory Verse

Don't let anyone look down on you because you are young.

~1 Timothy 4:12

What You Need

- duplicated page
- crayons

What to Do

After reviewing the story, give each child a copy of this page. Tell them that Timothy begins with the letter T. Repeat the T sound together. Have them circle the items on the page that begin with the letter T.

What to Say

Timothy grew up learning about God and His Son, Jesus. Timothy's mother and grandmother taught him about God when he was very little. He loved the Lord and wanted to help build His church. When he met Paul, a missionary, he wanted to help him, even though he was still just a young man. Do you think God could use you? What are some of the ways you can obey God?

Timothy

"Love"ly Flowers
♪ 1 Timothy 4:12; 2 Timothy 1:5-7; 3:14-15 ♫

Memory Verse

Don't let anyone look down on you because you are young.

~1 Timothy 4:12

What You Need

- duplicated page
- gift wrap
- safety scissors
- glue

What to Do

Give each child a copy of this page. Have several 2-3 inch squares of scrap gift wrap ready. Demonstrate how to cut out a heart by folding the paper in half and cutting the paper. Have the children cut out several of their own hearts. Help them glue the hearts onto the stems below to make "love"ly flowers.

What to Say

While Timothy was growing up, he enjoyed sitting with his mother and grandmother, learning all kinds of things. They taught him so much! But the most important thing that they taught him was about Jesus. Because Timothy listened to what his mother and grandmother taught him, he grew up to be a fine man who loved Jesus and told others about Him.

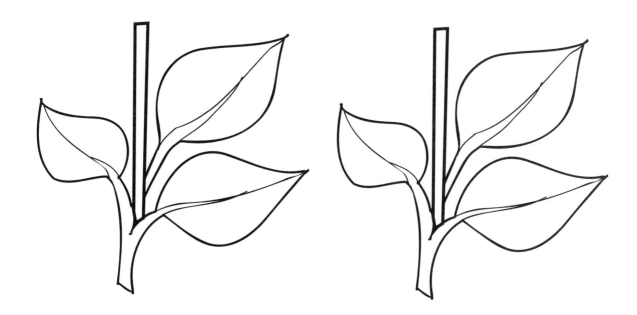

Timothy

Grow as You Learn
❧ 1 Timothy 4:12; 2 Timothy 1:5-7; 3:14-15 ❧

Memory Verse

And how from infancy you have known the holy Scriptures.

~2 Timothy 3:15

What You Need

- page 91
- safety scissors
- crayons

What to Do

Give each child a copy of the circle on page 91. Allow them to color it, but caution the students that the lines should still be visible because you will be cutting them. Show how to cut the circle out along the lines. Demonstrate how to hold it up from the center and watch it grow. (You will want to have extra copies available in case of cutting mistakes.)

What to Say

While growing up, Timothy listened carefully to what his mother, Eunice, and his grandmother, Lois, taught him about Jesus. God was able to use him to teach many other people about Jesus. Timothy grew into a fine young man. Can you think of anyone who was never a child? Of course not! We all grow! Even though grown-ups stop growing in their body, they can grow in their brains by learning. At your age, you are growing in your body and in your brain. Can you start learning about God now even though you are young?

Timothy

Listen to Your Mother!
♪ 1 Timothy 4:12; 2 Timothy 1:5-7; 3:14-15 ℅

Memory Verse

Continue in what you have learned.

~2 Timothy 3:14

What You Need

• no materials needed

What to Do

Explain to the children that you are going to play a game where they have to remember certain things that their mothers probably taught them. Ask them to imitate how they brush their teeth, wash their hands, put on their socks, eat their food, etc. To play the game, stand in front of the children and say, "My mother told me to wash my hands." Have everyone imitate this task after you have said it. Next, say, "My mother told me to wash my hands and brush my teeth." Have everyone imitate these two tasks after you have said them. Each time, add a task that the children have to remember and do them in order. The game ends when you run out of tasks or they can't remember the order in which you said them.

What to Say

All of his life, young Timothy was taught by his mother and grandmother. They taught him how to care for himself, and the difference between right and wrong. But the most important thing that they taught him was about Jesus. Paul told Timothy never to forget the things his mother taught him. His love for Jesus would help him the rest of his life.

Timothy

Memory Verse Choir

Memory Verse

God did not give us a spirit of timidity, but a spirit of power, of love and of self-discipline.
~2 Timothy 1:7

What You Need

• page 94
• glue
• craft sticks

What to Do

Before class, make two sets of number paddles by cutting out the number squares on page 94 and gluing them to craft sticks. Divide your class into four groups. Designate a leader for each group and give the leaders a number paddle. Teach each group their designated phrase: (1) "God did not give us a spirit of timidity," (2) "but a spirit of power," (3) "of love," (4) "and of self-discipline." Give the children definitions of timidity ("shyness") and self-discipline ("doing what is right"). Tell the children that when you hold up a number paddle that matches the number that their group leader is holding, they are to say their phrase. Start out slowly, holding up the numbers in order, then speed up. If your group catches on quickly, switch groups and have the children learn new phrases until all of the groups have learned all of the phrases. Then say the verse all together.

What to Say

Just because he was young does not mean that Timothy couldn't have an important role in building the new church. God gave him a special spirit, one of power and love to help him. No matter how old or young we are, with God's power and love, we can help accomplish great things, just like Timothy.

1	2
3	4

Timothy

Memory Verse

And how from infancy you have known the holy Scriptures.

~2 Timothy 3:15

What You Need

- duplicated page
- pencils
- crayons

What to Do

Copy a letter for each child. Help them write the name of the person they would like to give their letter/picture to. It can be for a parent, sibling, teacher or a special friend. In the blank space, they can draw a picture of the person helping them.

What to Say

Even though Timothy was just a young man, Paul took time to help him learn more about Jesus. Timothy had been eager to learn about Jesus ever since he was a little boy. Timothy was a great help to Paul when he was first building the church. Just as Paul wrote a letter to Timothy thanking him for his help and letting him know what a good job he was doing, we can write letters to people to thank them for helping us. Who has helped you get to know God the best? How has that person helped you?

Dear_____,

Thank you for helping me to learn about God.

Love,

_____